MW01002711

Living the
Spirit-Led Life

VOLUME
2

Living *the* Spirit-Led Life

For all who are led by the Spirit of God
are children of God. Romans 8:14

·····································
A 30-day Devotional Bible Study
for Individuals or Groups.
·····································

Dr. Larry Keefauver

CREATION
HOUSE
Orlando, FL

Living the Spirit-Led Life by Larry Keefauver

Published by Creation House
Strang Communications Company
600 Rinehart Road
Lake Mary, FL 32746

Web site: http://www.creationhouse.com

Unless otherwise noted, all Scripture quotations are the Holy Bible, New Living Translation, copyright © 1996. Used by permission of Tyndale House Publishers, Inc., Wheaton, IL 60189. All rights reserved.

Printed in the United States of America

ISBN 0-88419-471-X

78901234 87654321

Contents

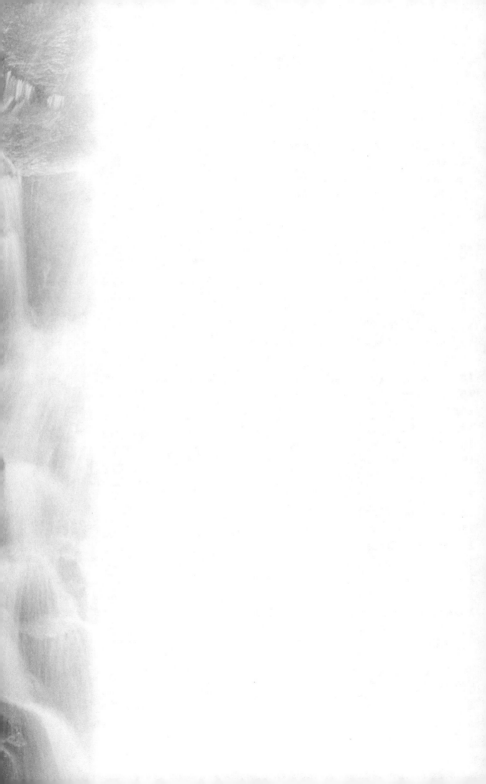

Introduction

Welcome to this devotional study on *Living the Spirit-led Life* that will assist you in welcoming the Holy Spirit into your life. This is one of eight devotional study guides related to the *Holy Spirit Encounter Bible*. Though not absolutely necessary, it is recommended that you obtain a copy of the *Holy Spirit Encounter Bible* for your personal use with this study guide. We make this recommendation because the same translation used in this guide, the *New Living Translation*, is also used in the *Holy Spirit Encounter Bible*.

It is also recommended that you choose the study guides in this series in the sequence that best meets your spiritual needs. So please don't feel that you must go through them in any particular order. Each study guide has been developed for individual, group, or class use.

Additional instruction has been included at the end of this guide for those desiring to use it in class or group settings.

Because the purpose of this guide is to help readers encounter the person of the Holy Spirit through the Scriptures, individuals going through it are invited to use it for personal daily devotional reading and study. Each daily devotional is structured to:

❖ Probe deeply into the Scriptures.

❖ Examine one's own personal relationship with the Holy Spirit.

❖ Discover biblical truths about the Holy Spirit.

❖ And, encounter the Person of the Holy Spirit continually in one's daily walk with God.

We pray this Bible study guide will serve you as an effective learning tool as you grow in fellowship with the wonderful third Person of the triune God—the Holy Spirit.

*H*e is the Holy Spirit, who leads into all truth. The world at large cannot receive him, because it isn't looking for him and doesn't recognize him. But you do, because he lives with you now and later will be in you (John 14:17).

It's always somewhat disconcerting during air travel when the pilot walks back through the passenger cabin of the plane. But he always has two backups. First, the plane's autopilot may be flying the plane as the pilot walks by your seat. Then there is always the co-pilot who can take over when needed.

In the Christian's life it's comforting to know we have the Holy Spirit as our autopilot, co-pilot, and computer system—all-in-one. He leads and teaches us in all truth. So in this devotional study we are going to discover how to yield to the Spirit's piloting, or, leading in our lives.

First, let's examine *what* the Spirit teaches and leads us into. *Truth!* And what is truth? Below is a list that includes definitions of absolute and relative truth mixed together. Check the statement(s) that refer to absolute truth:

_____ Truth is determined by the situation.

_____ Truth becomes fresh and flexible in every age.

_____ Truth is shaped and conditioned by love.

_____ Truth is what's right for all people.

_____ Truth is defined by God's nature and character.

_____ Truth is what feels right by each individual.

If your (only) check was placed next to the second to the last answer in the list above, you're right! Because absolute truth is defined by the nature and character of God. It is not determined by what people think or feel, but by God's unchanging truth as defined in His Person and in His Word. You can even see it in His creation's scientific record. Look up the following scriptures and jot down what they reveal about truth.

Deuteronomy 32:4 _____

Psalm 25:10, 26:3 _____

Psalm 43:3 _____

Isaiah 65:16 _____

John 1:14, 14:6 _____

Ephesians 4:21 _____

Hebrews 4:12 _____

1 Peter 1:22 _____

The Holy Spirit leads and guides us into the absolute truth, presence, purpose, and person, of God in Christ. He leads us in the way of the truth and life that are found in Jesus Christ (John 14:6). So throughout this devotional study we will discover how the Holy Spirit both leads and teaches us truth.

God's truth has been lived out through the Son of Man, Jesus (John 1:14), and revealed to us through His Spirit-breathed Word (2 Tim. 3:16; Eph. 6:17).

> *Truth is not what we think or feel are right. Truth is God's Word— lived out in time and space by Jesus, who demonstrated how we can be led by the Holy Spirit to do the will of the Father.*

Complete these sentences:

Truth is _____.

Truth is learned by _____.

Truth is lived when_____.

Ask Yourself . . .

❖ Do you try to make truth relative, or do you accept absolute truth?

❖ How has the Spirit been leading you in truth?

❖ What truth is the Spirit teaching you now?

Write a prayer asking God's Spirit to lead and teach you in His truth:

_____

_____

_____

*E*ach of you must turn from your sins [repent] and turn to God, and be baptized in the name of Jesus Christ for the forgiveness of your sins. Then you will receive the gift of the Holy Spirit (Acts 2:38).

No one can be led by the Holy Spirit until they repent. So repentance is the prerequisite to receiving God's gift of salvation through the Holy Spirit. Repentance surrenders self totally to God.

DAY 2
Starting With Repentance

Have you completely surrendered yourself to God and received Jesus Christ as your personal Lord and Savior? If not, do so now as you pray the following prayer aloud. If you have been born again, pray this again to simply reaffirm your faith:

Almighty God, I repent of my sins and surrender my life to You. I confess and believe that Jesus is Your Son the Christ, and my Savior and Lord. I ask for forgiveness through Jesus' sacrifice on the cross. Cleanse me through Jesus' shed blood. I will obey You in baptism and in all things. I ask for the gift of Your Holy Spirit. Thank You for saving me. Amen.

When you repent, you turn away from your old sinful lifestyle and receive power through the Holy Spirit to live a powerful new life in Christ, fully assured of eternal life.

> *Without repentance, the unsaved can never be saved. And without repentance, the saved who continue to sin can never experience the continual guidance and leading of the Holy Spirit.*

Read these scriptures, then summarize what they say about repentance and new life in Christ:

John 3:16 _____

2 Corinthians 5:17_____

Matthew 3:2,11_____

Mark 2:9–11_____

Luke 3:3 _____

Acts 3:9–11, 26:20 _____

2 Corinthians 7:9 _____

2 Peter 3:9 _____

We can't save ourselves (Rom. 5), nor can we direct our own lives. After repentance, we desperately need the gift of the indwelling Holy Spirit so we can know what to do and where to go in our lives. Take some time now to think about the areas of your life in which you hunger and thirst for the presence of God to renew, refresh, and lead you. Then write down the three most compelling areas:

1. _____

2. _____

3. _____

The Word promises that we will receive the Holy Spirit if we ask for Him. "If you sinful people know how to give good gifts to your children, how much more will your heavenly Father give the Holy Spirit to those who ask him" (Luke 11:13).

You may have been a born-again Christian (John 3:3) for years, but have been resisting the leading of God's Spirit. If you have, simply repent (1 John 1:9). Surrender yourself totally to God now and allow the tears of purifying repentance to flow through and flood your life.

Ask Yourself . . .

❖ What sin in your life stifles and hinders the Holy Spirit?

❖ Do you need to repent and surrender totally to the leading of the Holy Spirit?

❖ Will you cry out now for forgiveness and cleansing?

Write a prayer of repentance confessing any sin in your life that hinders the leading of God's Spirit in your life:

_____

_____

_____

*B*ecause we have these promises, dear friends, let us cleanse ourselves from everything that can defile our body or spirit. And let us work toward complete purity [holiness] because we fear God (2 Cor. 7:1).

DAY 3
The Purity of Holiness

Some apples look beautiful, pure, and edible from the outside, but are rotten in some places under the skin. As believers, our outward appearances may seem holy and pure, but inwardly we can have hidden, or rotten, areas of sin.

God looks on the heart of man's inward appearance (1 Sam. 16:7). He always looks "under" the skin.

> God desires inner purity and holiness.

Below is a portion of David's prayer of repentance from Psalm 51. <u>Underline</u> the parts which speak to your heart that you need to take to prayer:

> *Purify me from my sins, and I will be clean.*
> *Wash me and I will be whiter than snow.*
> *Oh, give me back my joy again.*
> *Do not banish me from your presence.*
> *Don't take your Holy Spirit from me.*
> *Restore to me again the joy of your salvation.*
> *Make me willing to obey you.*
> *The sacrifice you want is a broken spirit.*
> *A broken and repentant heart, O God, you will not despise.*

Holiness and purity mean to be set apart from sin, and dedicated, or consecrated, solely unto the Lord. So as Paul wrote in 2 Corinthians 7:1, we must cleanse ourselves from everything that defiles us. As the Holy Spirit begins to lead us into God's truth once we're born again, He gives us the desire and power to get rid of the sin that lies under our skin, and to purify our lives.

Check any of the following you know the Holy Spirit has been leading you to remove from your life to be pure and holy before God:

- ☐ Immorality
- ☐ Jealousy
- ☐ Pornography
- ☐ Gossip
- ☐ Hate
- ☐ Strife
- ☐ Addiction

- ☐ Lying
- ☐ Pride
- ☐ Lustful thoughts or desires
- ☐ Stealing or cheating
- ☐ Unforgiveness
- ☐ Idolatry
- ☐ Other_____

The Holy Spirit can't lead us when we continue to live unholy and impure lives. He gave us His freedom and power to live holy and pure. Read Romans 6:19–23, then complete the following sentences:

For me, holiness means that I must _____

_____.

To stay pure, I need _____

_____.

The things that lead to holiness that I must start doing are_____

_____.

Ask Yourself . . .

❖ Is holiness more important to you than your own desires? If not, why?

❖ What believers do you know who can help you be accountable to your walk of holiness?

Write a prayer inviting the Holy Spirit to convict and empower you to cleanse all impurity from your life:

_____

_____

_____

_____

*B*ut you are free from the power of sin and have become slaves of God. Now you do those things that lead to holiness and result in eternal life (Rom. 6:22).

DAY 4

The Fruit of Holiness

A Spirit-led walk is birthed in *being*, not by *doing.* The new Christian receives God's Spirit by being born again: "The truth is, no one can enter the Kingdom of God without *being* born of water and the Spirit" (John 3:5, italics added). Salvation is not earned, it is the free gift of God (Rom. 5; Eph. 2:8–10).

Being produces *doing.* And good deeds grow out of our lives as the result of God's Spirit at work in us. James says, *faith is dead without good deeds* (James 2:26). So read the following passages, then summarize those things we do as believers that produce holiness in our lives [John 15:5; Gal. 5:22; Rom. 12:3–21].

_____

_____

_____

_____

Holiness isn't something we achieve. It's not some lofty Christian goal we arrive at one day and say, "Here I am. I have finally attained 'holiness.'" No. Rather, we are made holy (sanctified) by the sacrificial blood of Jesus, by grace, to live in a righteous position of holiness (Rom. 1:16–17).

Read the following verses and list in the appropriate column what the verse indicates we either have left in the world, or who we are in Christ.

VERSE	What we have left in the world	Who we are in Christ
Deuteronomy 14:2		
2 Corinthians 5:17		
1 Peter 2:9		
Ephesians 1:11–14		
Ephesians 5:3–9		
Colossians 3:1–4		
Colossians 3:5–9		

Colossians 3:10–15 _____   _____

John 1:12–13   _____   _____

> *As a result of being made holy [set apart] by the shed blood of Christ on the cross, you are not only in the position, but also have the power to produce the good fruit of holiness.*

You *were* sanctified, are *being* sanctified and *will be* sanctified through the gift of God's grace in setting you apart. Imagine a carpet cleaning machine. When plugged into an electrical socket, it is in the position to work out its purpose. Turned on, it works out its purpose through the power flowing through it. So once it has been plugged in, turned on, and applied, the end result is a washed clean carpet.

Plugged into Christ, we are in a position of holiness. The power to produce good fruit flows from the gift of His Holy Spirit (John 15:8, 16). Then our good fruit shines in the world from which we have been set apart to bear holy witness to our holy God (Matt. 5:14–16).

Ask Yourself . . .

❖ What things that lead to holiness are you doing through the Spirit's power?

❖ What things do you need to stop doing that are producing impurity?

> *Write a prayer thanking Jesus Christ for His shed blood that made you holy and for His Spirit who keeps you holy through convicting and leading you:*

_____

_____

_____

_____

_____

_____

*F*irst, however, let me tell you about something else that is better than any of them [spiritual gifts]! . . . There are three things that will endure—faith, hope, and love—and the greatest of these is love (1 Cor. 12:31, 13:13).

DAY 5

Love is the Greatest

Years ago a certain heavyweight boxing champion would triumphantly parade around the ring after a victory proclaiming, "I am the greatest! I am the greatest!" His superior skills and pride motivated his claim.

But in the spiritual realm, love *is* the greatest work of God's Spirit within us. Because God's Spirit—not pride—produces God's self-sacrificing kind of love (*agape*). It is not arrogant and gives no place to human might.

> *God's love at work in us seeks the best for others around us and is not conditioned by their response.*

God's agape love says, "If others are ungrateful, I still love them. If they resist or hate me, I still love." List three persons who need God's unconditional love, then write down God's best you are wanting for them:

Name   **God's best for them**

1._____   _____

2._____   _____

3._____   _____

God's Spirit within us produces the fruit of His unconditional love in our lives (Gal. 5:22). Match the people we are to show His love to with the correct scripture by drawing a line from one to the other.

People We Are To Love

Friends

Spouses

Neighbors

Jesus

God

Other believers

Enemies

Texts

John 14:23–24

Deuteronomy 6:5

John 15:12–16

Ephesians 5:25–28

Romans 12:10

Luke 6:35

Mark 12:31

Now give yourself a little test. What is the most important way that faith expresses itself? Below is a list of the ways. Put them in order based on your beliefs from 1 (the most important) to 5 (the least important on the list).

_____ Doing good works

_____ Being kind

_____ Serving others

_____ Loving everyone

_____ Preaching good news

All of the above are important, but love is at the top of the list because Paul wrote, "What is important is faith expressing itself in love" (Gal. 5:6). Everything else on the list are outward expressions of love. They can even be empty and meaningless expressions rooted in the "have-nots" of law. But love fulfills the law (Rom. 13:8).

Love Check-up Check List
Check the ways you are comfortable expressing love for others, and circle the ways you aren't:

❏ Forgiving	❏ Hugs	❏ A touch	❏ A look
❏ A note	❏ A phone call	❏ Gifts	❏ Serving
❏ Sharing	❏ Visiting	❏ Correction	❏ Sharing Jesus
❏ Doing something for them		❏ Saying, "I love you"	
❏ Speaking the truth in love		❏ Other:_____	

Ask Yourself . . .

❖ Who is hardest for you to love?

❖ What do you need to do to be reconciled to him or her?

Write a prayer expressing your love for God the Father, Son, and Holy Spirit, asking them to shed their love abroad to others through your life:

_____

_____

_____

*S*o now I [Jesus] *am giving you a new command-*
ment: Love each other. Just as I have loved you, you
should love each other. Your love for one another
will prove to the world that you are my disciples (John
13:34–35).

At times, the world must be confused by the picture
the church paints for them. On the one hand, we
claim to love everyone and serve a Savior who so
loved the world that He died to save it. But on the
other, the world witnesses our church splits, attacks,
dissension, and strife.

DAY 6
Known By Our Fruit

> *Love for one another in the body proves*
> *to the world that we follow Jesus.*

Offenses in the body hinder God's love. And if we can't love one another, we
certainly can't love the lost and win them to Christ! An offense is a hurt that
you have chosen to harbor in your heart. Hate, anger, and offenses arise when
we have:

❖ Unfulfilled expectations
❖ Unmet needs
❖ Unresolved anger

Read Matthew 5:21–26, 7:1–5, then list below anyone with whom you have an
offense. Some may have actually intended to hurt you. Others may still be
unaware that anything is wrong. Write down their names and identify the
offense.

Name	Hurt or Offense
_____	_____
_____	_____
_____	_____

Now read the following passages, then jot down how we are to handle hurts
and offenses:

Matthew 5:23–25 _____

Matthew 6:14–15 _____

Matthew 18:21–22 _____

Mark 11:26 _____

Romans 12:14–21 _____

We can say that we love others, but the proof of our love is accepting forgiveness (1 John 3:11–24). When we obey God and forgive others, we confirm that the Spirit's love dwells in us. Still, forgiving takes effort on our part, because we must:

- ❖ Admit the hurt, offense, hate, or bitterness in us
- ❖ Confess it to God
- ❖ Be reconciled to the other person
- ❖ Seek prayer from other Christians and the elders for healing
- ❖ Let go of the past and determine not to bring up the past ever again

Think of one person you need to forgive. Now look at the above steps and complete the following sentences:

1. What has kept you from forgiving this person is _____
_____.

2. The next step you need to take is _____
_____.

3. Persons you need to pray with you are _____
_____.

Ask Yourself . . .

- ❖ How does the fruit of love express itself daily in you?

- ❖ What do you need to do daily to forgive others?

Write a prayer confessing any hurts or offenses that releases those involved into God's forgiveness:

_____

_____

*S*o I advise you to live according to your new life in the Holy Spirit. Then you won't be doing what your sinful nature craves (Gal. 5:16).

DAY 7

New Life in the Spirit

Living the Spirit-led life means that you have been freed from past sin and guilt. If you feel guilty about the past once your new life begins as a new creature in Christ, it's because you want to, not because you're guilty. In fact, continuing to hold onto the old denies the power of the new thing God is doing in you as a new creation (2 Cor. 5:17).

If you are alive in the new life of Christ, you have been set free from your old sinful nature to live victoriously in the Spirit. "And the Spirit gives us desires that are opposite from what the sinful nature desires. These two forces are constantly fighting each other, and your choices are never free from this conflict. But when you are directed by the Holy Spirit, you are no longer subject to the law" (Gal. 5:17–18).

What the Spirit desires truly is in direct opposition to the sinful nature of the flesh. To help you better understand this, look over the "works of the flesh" list below from Galatians 5:19–21 and write down the opposite of each sinful desire:

My old sinful nature desired	Led by the Spirit, I desire the opposite, which is . . .
Sexual immorality	_____
Impure thoughts	_____
Eagerness for lustful pleasure	_____
Idolatry	_____
Participation in demonic activity	_____
Quarreling	_____
Hostility	_____
Jealousy	_____
Outbursts of anger	_____
Selfish ambition	_____
Divisions	_____
The feeling that everyone is wrong except those in your own little group.	_____

Envy   _____

Drunkenness   _____

Wild parties   _____

Other sins   _____

The opposites you wrote down can be summarized in the list of the Spirit's fruit recorded in Galatians 5:22–23. All of these fruits are in us because the Spirit indwells us. But they need to grow, mature and ripen in our daily lives. Each fruit below has been labeled as a fruit of the Spirit. Shade each piece of fruit to the degree that it has matured in your life. For example, if you exhibit patience about half the time, shade that piece to 50 percent:

Living the Spirit-led life means that you are always growing and maturing in Christ.

> *The Spirit-led believer has the potential for every one of the Spirit's fruits to manifest at all times, in all situations, with all people.*

However, the fruit of the Spirit will only manifest to the degree that we yield to His direction and control.

Ask Yourself . . .

❖ What in you still needs to fully yield to the power of the Holy Spirit?

❖ How is the fruit of the Spirit growing and maturing in your life?

Write a prayer asking God's Spirit to empower you to grow and mature in the fruit of the Spirit:

_____

_____

_____

*F*or the commandments against adultery and mur-
der and stealing and coveting—and any other
commandment—are all summed up in this one
commandment: "Love your neighbor as yourself." Love
does no wrong to anyone, so love satisfies all of God's
requirements (Rom. 13:9–10).

Love: Fulfilling the Law

The Spirit's fruit of love is rooted in God's nature:
"But anyone who does not love does not know
God—for God is love" (1 John 4:8).

God's love is defined by the Greek word *agape.*
Agape means "unconditional, sacrificial love that
seeks God's best for others." Other kinds of love are:

> *Philos*—brotherly or sisterly love that draws people together to accomplish a
> common goal. Teams and partnerships most often reflect *philos* love.

> *Storge*—natural affection among family members.

> *Eros*—physical or sexual attraction and desire.

> *While various forms of human love may be a part of our love for another
> person, the deepest, lasting and most unselfish type of love is agape.*

Put an *x* on each line that represents where you are with love:

I love . . .

All people	Select people
Unconditionally	Conditionally
Unselfishly	Selfishly
All the time	Periodically
Joyfully	Dutifully

If you found yourself marking more in the right "human love" column, then
agape flows with difficulty in your life. But there is good news. You aren't the

source of God's *agape,* nor is His source limited. God's Spirit produces an endless and limitless fruit of love. In fact, the more we love, the more God's love flows in and through us by the power of His Spirit.

Below is a passage from the Bible's preeminent love chapter—1 Corinthians 13. Underline each quality of God's *agape* love that is bearing fruit in your life, and circle each quality that needs significant cultivation by His Spirit.

Love is patient and kind.

Love is not jealous or boastful or proud or rude.

Love does not demand its own way.

Love is not irritable,

and it keeps no record of when it has been wronged.

It is never glad about injustice

but rejoices whenever the truth wins out.

Love never gives up,

never loses faith,

is always hopeful,

and endures through every circumstance.

—1 Corinthians 13:4–7

Ask Yourself . . .

❖ In what ways does God's Spirit want you to increase your love for those around you who are hard to love?

❖ Who needs your love today? How will you express it to them?

Write a prayer thanking God for His selfless, sacrificial agape love and the power given by His Spirit that enables you to love others:

_____

_____

_____

_____

_____

*T*herefore, since we have been made right in God's sight by faith, we have peace with God because of what Jesus Christ our Lord has done for us (Rom. 5:1).

Because the Spirit's fruit of peace fills us with His inner peace regardless of the storms around us, our peace is firmly rooted in the confident presence of Him. It isn't affected by what we see around us, but by Who is living in us. The indwelling Holy Spirit maintains our peace with God through the shed blood of Jesus Christ.

Read the following passages, then jot down what they say about our everlasting peace with God through Jesus Christ:

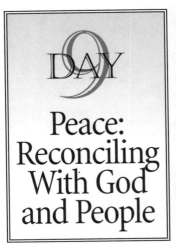

DAY 9

Peace: Reconciling With God and People

Isaaiah 9:6 _____

John 14:27 _____

John 20:21 _____

Romans 5:10, 14:7 _____

2 Corinthians 13:11 _____

Colossians 1:20–21 _____

2 Corinthians 5:18 _____

> *True peace is being reconciled with God.*

God's peace flows as a river of peace (Isa. 48:18) from within you to bring peace to the lives of others. The river of God's peaceful Spirit flows in and through His believers into everyone they know with refreshing and renewing. But we can't have lasting peace with others until we have inner peace. And we can't have inner peace without receiving the fruit of peace from God.

Take some time now to think of those with whom you don't have a peaceful relationship. Who are they? Think about how you can bring the fruit of peace into your relationship with them.

Now read Romans 12:18 and list any people from whom you are feeling alienated. Then draw a line from their names to the action(s) you need to take to be reconciled:

Name	**Reconciling Actions**
_____	Write a letter
_____	Make a phone call
_____	Visit them
_____	Ask forgiveness
_____	Forgive them
_____	Humble yourself
_____	Forget the past
_____	Other:_____

Anyone who doesn't bear the fruit of peace in their relationships will experience inner turmoil and restlessness inside. So if you have difficulty making peace with others, stop blaming them and look inside of yourself. Are you at peace with God? Are you at peace with your past?

Ask Yourself . . .

❖ How can you release the Spirit's fruit of peace in your life today?

❖ How will you reach out to those with whom you are alienated?

Write a prayer thanking Jesus for giving you the Spirit's peace, and His power to be a peacemaker:

_____

_____

*B*e humble and gentle. Be patient with each other, making allowance for each other's faults because of your love (Eph. 4:2).

10 DAY

Patience: Enduring in the Spirit

Patience means to endure, remain steadfast, and persevere. In other words, to be patient means to finish anything as strong or stronger than you started it. Some people start strong, then either drop out, quit, or finish weak. But the Holy Spirit is a strong finisher. He will always empower us to finish strong for Jesus through the fruit of patience in our faith.

The Spirit's fruit of patience can be witnessed in both our relationship with Christ and in our relationships with one other. Take some time now to think back to the first few months or years that you were a new Christian. How does your life in the Spirit now compare to then?

Think of some Christians you have known through the years who have finished strong for Christ. Jot down their names, and one quality of their spiritual walk that is an example for you:

Name   **Exemplary Quality**

_____   _____

_____   _____

_____   _____

Has your faith and spiritual walk grown stronger over the years? Has your endurance, patience and perseverance strengthened? Is your commitment to finishing strong for Jesus Christ stronger now than it has ever been?

> *We are able to persevere because God is a patient God who waits on us. His Spirit gives us the strength to endure.*

Read the following scriptures, then jot down how God perseveres with us:

Romans 2:3–4 _____

Romans 9:22–24_____

1 Timothy 1:15–16 _____

James 5:10 _____

2 Peter 3:15 _____

Our patient Lord is shaping us by His Spirit into His image (2 Cor. 3:16–18). That means we are becoming patient like Him, and that we have the ability to be patient with others (2 Tim. 3:10, 4:2; Heb. 6:12). Below are a number of words that describe His patience. Circle the ones that apply to you and underline those that need His cultivation:

Perseverance	Longsuffering	Waiting
Endurance	Forbearance	Finishing strong

Are you willing to wait on the Lord for His timing and will in every circumstance and relationship in your life? Or do you get impatient—trying to move ahead of God or by trying to force something to happen that is not His will?

Ask Yourself . . .

❖ What is the Holy Spirit doing in you right now to equip you to finish strong?

❖ In what situations is it difficult for you to wait upon the Lord?

Write a prayer asking for the fruit of patience to grow in your life:

_____

_____

_____

_____

_____

I nstead, be kind to each other, tenderhearted, forgiving one another, just as God through Christ has
forgiven you (Eph. 4:32).

DAY 11

Kindness: Forgiving One Another

A wise marriage counselor was once asked, "What is the most important counsel you give to couples?" He replied, "Be kind to one another." But at times, people may be kinder to strangers and even pets than they are to those they love. At the root of kindness is wanting the best for another person. So kindness means putting another's needs and concerns above our own. Kindness, mercy, and gentleness all work together in the Spirit's fruit of kindness.

Read each of the following scriptures, then jot down how kindness is expressed in the Spirit-led life:

Psalm 41:1; Proverbs 28:8 _____

Psalm 116:5, 148:8_____

Proverbs 3:3; 16:24 _____

Acts 20:24_____

1 Corinthians 13:4 _____

Kindness promptly forgives. It refuses to carry grudges or seek vengeance. Kindness cares and honors others without a thought of gratitude or reward.

> *Kindness serves a need even before it is expressed.*

Spirit-led believers are known for their expressions of kindness. The Spirit will lead us to deliberately be kind to others.

Take some time to think of five people who have been deliberately kind to you and how they showed their kindness:

Name   **Act of Kindness**

_____   _____

_____   _____

_____   _____

_____   _____

_____   _____

Now consider all the ways God has demonstrated His kindness toward you. List the ways you can think of that God has shown His kindness to you then look up these scriptures to add to your list: (Ps. 145:8; Rom. 2:4, 5:20–2; Eph. 1:6–8, 2:7; 1 Tim. 1:14)

God's Kindness Is . . .

_____

_____

_____

It is often harder to be kind to those who are unkind to you. So think of those now who are unkind to you and decide:

1. To forgive.

2. To forget the offense.

3. To love.

4. To show kindness.

Now circle the act of kindness above that is hardest for you and name an unkind person you need most to be kind to. Decide to start with the hardest step and do all the rest. Because God has been kind and merciful to us, we can be kind and merciful to others.

Ask Yourself . . .

❖ Who has a need right now that you can meet?

❖ What kind act can you do soon for one who is unkind to you?

Write a prayer thanking God for His kindness toward you and for the inspiration of His Spirit to be kind to others:

_____

_____

_____

*F*or the Kingdom of God is not a matter of what we eat or drink, but of living a life of goodness and peace and joy in the Holy Spirit (Rom. 14:17).

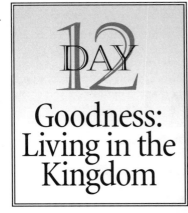

Goodness above all else speaks of integrity. Integrity is who you are and what you do when no one else is looking. Do you have integrity in the secret of your bedroom? Do you have integrity on a trip away from everyone back in your home town?

Have you ever smelled fresh bread baking? The whole house is filled with the good aroma of the bread. And, that first bite into a hot slice of homemade bread is so gooooood! Think of integrity that way. Not only does a person of godly integrity "smell" good in all appearances, they also "taste" good, spiritually. When you get to know them they are good from the inside out.

The foremost ingredient of goodness, is integrity. Below is a loaf of bread with some slices cut from it. Read the following Scriptures then write on each slice some of the qualities revealed to you about integrity. (1 Chron. 29:17, 2 Chron. 19:9; Job 1:1, 2:3, 8:20; Ps. 25:1, 26:1, 101:2, 119:1; Prov. 2:21, 10:9, 20:7; Titus 2:7)

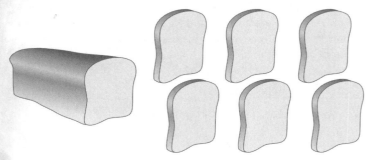

A second ingredient of goodness is moral virtue. But the measure of goodness can never be ourselves or others. Whether or not we are moral or good is based on a comparison with the character of God, not others. And compared to God, "No one is good—not even one" (Rom. 3:10). So when the Holy Spirit convicts us of bad thoughts or actions, the basis on which He convicts us is the nature of goodness in God.

When examining your moral virtue based on God's nature, how good are you? Listening to the Holy Spirit, evaluate yourself on a scale of 1 (very good) to 5 (very bad). Circle the appropriate number:

Truthfulness	1	2	3	4	5
Moral purity	1	2	3	4	5
Faithfulness	1	2	3	4	5
Loving others	1	2	3	4	5
Humility	1	2	3	4	5
Serving	1	2	3	4	5

> *Where we lack goodness and virtue, the Holy Spirit fills the gap.*

Now for the good news.

It's not by our own strength or effort, but by the Holy Spirit that we are able to live a good life (Zech. 4:6), because apart from God's Spirit, there is no goodness.

Ask Yourself . . .

❖ How is God's goodness a standard of righteousness for every decision you make?

❖ How does God's Spirit hold you accountable as a person of integrity?

Write a prayer asking the Holy Spirit to keep you accountable to His standard of goodness:

_____

_____

_____

_____

_____

*W*e proudly tell God's other churches about your endurance and faithfulness in all the persecutions and hardships you are suffering (2 Thess. 1:4).

Remaining steadfast and faithful during times of persecution and hardship can be very difficult. When we are persecuted for the sake of righteousness, we are to rejoice (Matt. 5:10–12). Have you decided to follow Jesus, no matter what the trial or cost? If you have, the Spirit's fruit of faithfulness will help you pay the price.

DAY 13
Faithfulness: Persevering Through Trials

Trials test our true loyalties. When a spouse is unfaithful in marriage or a best friend stabs a friend in the back, marriage vows and loyalty are really put to the test.

One of the best examples of faithfulness in Scripture is Job's perseverance through his trials. "We give great honor to those who endure under suffering. Job is an example of a man who endured patiently. From his experience we see how the Lord's plan finally ended in good, for he is full of tenderness and mercy" (James 5:11).

Could you remain faithful to God no matter what happened? Check those things that would severely test your loyalty to God:

❑ The untimely death of a loved one

❑ The loss of your home

❑ Suddenly becoming poor and destitute

❑ Church members turning against you

❑ A best friend betraying you

❑ Other: _____

The Holy Spirit empowers us to be faithful to God because He is *always* faithful and merciful to us. No matter how many times we've sinned against God or rejected His will, He still loves and forgives us. Read the following Scriptures then complete the sentences below:

[Exod. 34:6, Deut. 7:9, 32:4; 1 Chron. 16:34,41; Ps. 31:5,]

God's faithfulness is_____

_____

[Josh. 23:8; 1 Kings 15:14; Ps. 18:25, 25:10, 91:4, 103:18]

I am faithful to God when_____

_____.

The tendency of our sinful nature is to displace our faithfulness to God with a counterfeit faithfulness to religion, institutions, doctrines or people. While loyalty to people and institutions may be admirable and virtuous, when we put them ahead of God, it becomes idolatry.

> *The Spirit at work in us helps us stay faithful to God and to be a promise keeper with others.*

Because God is faithful in keeping His promises to us (2 Cor. 1:20), we keep our promises to spouses, children, family, friends, and others. Are you a faithful promise keeper mirroring God's nature in your words and actions?

Put an *x* on the line where you are:

I make promises

| Seriously | Thoughtlessly | Recklessly |

I keep my vows

| Always | Sometimes | Never |

I fulfill my contracts

| Completely | | Incompletely |

I keep promises

| Faithfully | | Randomly |

Ask Yourself . . .

❖ What promises have you made that you still need to fulfill? When will you keep them?

❖ From whom do you need to seek forgiveness for breaking a promise?

Write a prayer thanking God's Spirit for helping you remain steadfastly faithful to Him and for helping you make and keep promises:

_____

_____

*S*ince God chose you to be the holy people whom he loves, you must clothe yourselves with tenderhearted mercy, kindness, humility, gentleness, and patience (Col. 3:12).

Gentleness: Humbling Ourselves

Gentleness or, meekness is an intrinsic trait in God's holy nature. So when we are led by the Spirit, pride has no place in our lives. In fact, pride gives Satan a foothold to attack us and lead us astray.

What does gentleness look like? Just look at Jesus. Read Philippians 2:1–11 then write beside the cross below all the attitudes and qualities that are revealed about gentle humility:

The greatest obstacle to gentleness in us is pride, because pride looks out for number one. It seeks personal glory above serving others. Pride desires all attention to be focused on self. Examine yourself. When does pride well up inside of you to devour the fruit of gentleness? Check the times that most tempt you to boast in your self:

❑ Accomplishing a goal

❑ The praise of others

❑ Receiving an honor

❑ Overcoming a past failure

❑ Having a new idea that impresses others

❑ Other: _____

The fruit of gentleness produces unselfishness. It purges selfish motives to give us Jesus' Philippians 2 perspective in our serving and giving. Gentleness moves us to serve because Jesus is the Suffering Servant. It moves us to give because God gives. Gentleness inspires us to comfort because the Spirit comforts us.

At times, others even try to manipulate us because they misinterpret our gentleness as weakness.

But gentleness never implies weakness. There is controlled strength in it. Jesus was the most gentle and humble person who ever lived, yet His strength as the Anointed One defeated the power of sin and death. Gentleness derives strength from the Holy Spirit, not from human ability. Read 2 Corinthians 12:8–10. Then summarize in one sentence the source of Paul's strength:

_____

_____

> *Gentleness refuses to use personal power or position to accomplish God's will.*

Gentleness submits to the Spirit's leading in every relationship and circumstance. Read the following Scriptures then jot down the blessings for showing God's gentleness:

Psalm 22:26, 25:9 _____

Psalm 37:11, 76:9 _____

Psalm 149:4 _____

Isaiah 29:19 _____

James 1:21 _____

Ask Yourself . . .

❖ In what situations or relationships do you need to surrender your own strength and control to rely completely on the Spirit's gentle. humility?

❖ With whom do you need to be gentle?

Write a prayer asking God's Spirit to shatter your pride and fill you with His fruit of gentleness:

_____

_____

_____

K nowing God leads to self-control. Self-control leads to patient endurance, and patient endurance leads to godliness (2 Peter 1:6).

DAY 15
Self-control: Disciplining Self

The Spirit-led life is directed, or, controlled, by the Spirit. The Christian who is out of control should love it. Why? Because our spiritual walk is not about us being in control, but about surrendering all control to the Holy Spirit. He is the One who knows best how to live out the days of our lives.

The Spirit's desire is birthed within us out of an intimate relationship with the Father to put self under His control. In the Spirit-led life, the Holy Spirit disciplines, teaches, and corrects us. So self-control doesn't arise from our personal determination or commitment to do right. Self-control grows out of knowing God.

We learn patient endurance and godliness under the Spirit's discipline and control. How do we learn? Through the Spirit's leading and thirst for His spiritual disciplines. A spiritual discipline is a Spirit-led way of deepening our relationship with the Father out of which we are directed to live righteously with others.

Below is a list of some of the Spirit's disciplines that teach us self-control. Check the spiritual disciplines that are a regular part of your life and circle those that need to grow and develop:

❏ Bible reading and study   ❏ Prayer and intercession

❏ Worship   ❏ Witnessing

❏ Stewardship and giving   ❏ Meditating on God's Word

❏ Silence and stillness before God ❏ Christian service

❏ Discipling others   ❏ Praise

❏ Solitude—being alone with God   ❏ Reading Christian books

❏ Christian fellowship   ❏ Other:

The Holy Spirit produces the fruit of self-control in our lives. That means we are disciplined by Him in the things of the Spirit and that every aspect of our lives is under His control. Now examine your life. Circle the following areas that need to come under the Spirit's complete control:

Thoughts	Feelings	Tongue	Expectations
Desires	Motives	Attitudes	Eating habits
What I see	What I touch	What I hear	

Other:_____

The Holy Spirit's fruit of self-control gives us the discipline to be crucified with Christ (Gal. 2:20). And when we are crucified with Christ, godliness, holiness, and servanthood direct our life.

Ask Yourself . . .

❖ In what area of your life is the Spirit teaching you self-control at this moment?

❖ When you get out of the way, what is the Spirit doing in and through you?

Write a prayer thanking the Spirit for taking control of your self:

_____

_____

_____

_____

_____

*B*ut now we have been released from the law, for we died with Christ, and we are no longer captive to its power. Now we can really serve God, not in the old way by obeying the letter of the law, but in the new way, by the Spirit (Rom. 7:6).

One of the greatest threats to the Spirit-led life is legalism. Legalism is carnal man's way of reducing God's Word to laws that can be both interpreted and implemented by human strength.

But God's Word is not a dead law. It is a living covenant that describes our relationship with Him, and people. Paul writes, "He [God] is the one who has enabled us to represent his new covenant. This is a covenant, not of written laws, but of the Spirit. The old way ends in death; in the new way, the Holy Spirit gives life" (2 Cor. 3:6).

Have you been trying to obey laws instead of living in the Spirit? Have you been bound by a spirit of legalism? Below is a list of traits that show the contrast between legalistic religion and life in the Spirit. Underline every statement that currently fits you:

Religious Legalism	Life in the Spirit
Controlling	Liberating
Motivated by guilt	Motivated by love
Pleases people	Pleases God
Judgmental	Accepting
Critical	Affirming
Indoctrinates	Instructs
Punishes	Corrects
Tears down	Edifies
Focuses on works	Focuses on grace
Slavery	Servanthood

If you underlined more statements in the legalism column than you did in the life in the Spirit column, take a moment right now to read through Romans 7:4, then pray this prayer aloud:

Lord Jesus, you have released me from the Law. I know that I can't earn salvation or Your favor. So I accept Your grace and saving death for me on the Cross. I die with You and declare liberty from the power of the Law. I desire to serve You, not by obeying laws, but by living in Your Spirit. Amen.

Legalism attempts to fix the sinful nature, while the Holy Spirit convicts and purifies through His presence in the new creation (2 Cor. 5:17). Why try to fix what's old when you can have a brand new nature in Christ?

The Spirit's way of life empowers us to fulfill the law by loving God and others (Rom. 13:10).

> *Life in the Spirit does not consist of a list of "do's and don'ts." It consists of His loving presence overflowing our hearts (Rom. 5:5).*

Read Jeremiah 31:33–34, then paraphrase this Scripture in your own written words over this heart:

Ask Yourself . . .

❖ Are you living by law or in the Spirit? In what areas of your life does the spirit of religion and legalism need to be broken?

❖ How can you encourage other believers to live in the Spirit and to avoid legalism?

Write a prayer praising Christ for setting you free from the do's and don'ts of the law into the overflowing grace of the Spirit's love:

_____

_____

_____

_____

_____

*S*o now there is no condemnation for those who belong to Christ Jesus. For the power of the life-giving Spirit has freed you through Christ from the power of sin that leads to death (Rom. 8:1–2).

Day 17 — Living Free

False condemnation produces a feeling of guilt for something that has already been forgiven. Satan is the accuser of the saints (Rev. 12). But he can't put a Christian under valid condemnation because every past sin of the born-again believer has been forgiven through the shed blood of Christ.

Still, some Christians choose to live under Satan's condemnation. They choose to listen to Satan's lies and the guilt of their own hearts (1 John 3:20–21). But the life-giving Spirit of God has set us free from all condemnation.

Are you feeling under condemnation right now? Examine yourself by answering the following questions:

For what do you feel condemned? _____

Who do you think is condemning you? (Satan, others, self) _____

Why are you accepting the condemnation? _____

Jesus declared you to be not guilty through the Cross! You have been set free from the power of sin to live in the power of the Holy Spirit!

Below is a list of some of things the power of the life-giving Spirit of God does for you. Check His manifestations that you have encountered:

❏ Freedom from past sin and guilt

❏ Joy in the Spirit

❏ The gifts of the Spirit

❏ The fruit of the Spirit

❏ Cleansing, healing, purification, and sanctification (holiness) by the Spirit

❏ A release from low self-concept

❏ Freedom from fear, depression, or anger

❏ Other:_____

The liberty and freedom that come through His Spirit empower you to live abundantly in Christ. Read these Scriptures then complete the sentences below: (John 8:32,35; Rom. 6:18; 1 Cor. 1:30, 7:22,32; 2 Cor. 3:17; Gal. 4:12. 5:1–3; Eph. 1:7; Col. 2:20; 1 Tim. 2:6)

How did Jesus set you free? _____

_____.

From what have you been set free? _____

_____.

For what have you been set free?_____

_____.

The believer's freedom in the Spirit is not a license to sin (Rom. 6:1). It is the Spirit's life-giving power that enables you to do what God desires in and through you. So cherish your freedom brought about by the shed blood of Jesus. Live in it for His glory to set other captives free (Isa. 61).

Ask Yourself . . .

❖ Is there anything in your past that you need to be set free from? If so, what is it? Will you ask the Spirit to break that bondage immediately?

❖ Are you putting others under any condemnation? If so, will you ask the Spirit to set you free from a judgmental or critical spirit?

Write a prayer asking God's Spirit to set you free from Satan's false condemnation, and for God's empowerment to share the good news of Christ's liberty with others:

_____

_____

_____

_____

_____

*B*ut you are not controlled by your sinful nature. You are controlled by the Spirit if you have the Spirit of God living in you (Rom. 8:9).

DAY 18
Spirit Controlled

Spirit-led Christians aren't spiritual puppets. God created us with free wills and inspired us to be creative. So there is no manipulation or coercion in the spirit-controlled life. Rather, there is an empowered freedom to be all that God has created us to be.

It is sin that seeks to manipulate and enslave us. The unsaved may protest that they are "free," but sin's subtle control motivates their every thought and action. Sin is not a doctrine. It is a diabolical force that seeks to control through deception, denial, and addiction. In fact, sin is the deadliest addiction! It is the ruination of the good.

The Holy Spirit delivers you from sin's slavery into the freedom of being God's own child. Read Galatians 4:6 then describe in our own words what it means to be a child of God:

_____

_____

The control of God's Spirit empowers us to live freely in His grace. Below are a number of attributes that contrast the way sin and the Spirit operate in the controlling of our lives. Check each line that indicates one influencing you now:

Sin controls through . . .	**The Spirit controls with . . .**
❏ Lies	❏ Truth
❏ Addiction	❏ Freedom
❏ Coercion	❏ Guidance
❏ Fear	❏ Trust
❏ Guilt	❏ Forgiveness
❏ Hate	❏ Love
❏ Manipulation	❏ Free choice
❏ Denial	❏ Facing reality
❏ Selfishness	❏ Selflessness
❏ Threats	❏ God's promises
❏ Worldly knowledge and reason	❏ Godly wisdom

You may be thinking control is control no matter what the source. But the truth of the matter is, true freedom only comes through the control of the Holy Spirit. Only He knows God's best for you. Only He has the power to help you break every bondage and defeat every addiction. Only He has the wisdom and counsel to help you plan for the future. So whose control would you rather be under—sin's, your own, or the Spirit's? The choice is yours.

When the Spirit isn't in control, we are powerless to act or think properly. Complete these sentences:

When sin controls me, I_____

_____.

When I try to take control, I _____

_____.

When the Spirit is in control, I _____

_____.

Ask Yourself . . .

❖ Who controls you, your family, your church, your work?

❖ What is your greatest fear in surrendering complete control to the Holy Spirit?

Write a prayer giving complete control of your life to the Holy Spirit:

_____

_____

_____

_____

_____

F or if you keep on following it [your sinful nature], you will perish. But if through the power of the Holy Spirit you turn from it and its evil deeds, you will live. For all who are led by the Spirit of God are the children of God. So you should not be like cowering, fearful slaves. You should behave like God's very own children, adopted into his family—calling Him "Father, dear Father." For his Holy Spirit speaks to us deep in our hearts and tells us that we are God's children (Rom. 8:13–16).

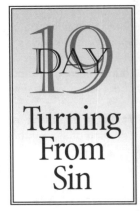

Day 19
Turning From Sin

To repent is to turn from sin. So when you repent, you make a deliberate choice to be led by the Spirit instead of your own sinful nature.

The result of following sin is death (1 Cor. 15:56). But no person can break free from the power of sin to experience victory over darkness in his own strength. Each of us needs the power of the Holy Spirit to break sin's bondage in our lives.

Are you facing bondages in your life that need to be broken? Is there sin you need to repent of and turn from? Below is a list of bondages. Check any that you need to ask the Spirit to help you turn from today:

_____Financial bondage	_____Sexual addiction
_____Overeating or gluttony	_____Laziness
_____Sin habits	_____Unclean thoughts
_____Racial prejudice	_____Religious traditions or legalism
_____Past failures	

Your identity in Christ as God's child has set you free from the past because you are a new creation. Take some time now to discover who you are as God's child. Read each of the following scriptures describing your identity in Christ, then jot down what they say about you:

As a Child of God	**I am . . .**
John 1:12	_____
John 15:15	_____
Romans 5:1	_____
1 Corinthians 3:16	_____
1 Corinthians 6:19–20	_____

1 Corinthians 12:27   _____

Ephesians 1:1   _____

Ephesians 1:5   _____

Colossians 1:14   _____

Colossians 2:10   _____

Life in the Spirit gives us the assurance of being both significant and secure in Christ. The Holy Spirit removes our insecurities and lack of confidence. Connect the following Scriptures that speak about security and significance with the right description of who you are in Christ by drawing a line from every passage to its appropriate match:

God's Word	**In Christ, I am . . .**
John 15:16	At peace with God
Eph. 2:6	Saved
John 15:5	Bearing fruit
1 Corinthains 12:27	A saint
John 15:15	Free from condemnation
Colossians 2:10	Complete and whole
Romans 5:1	Jesus' friend
Ephesians 1:1	Part of Christ's body
Romans 10:9	Seated with Christ

Ask Yourself . . .

❖ What sin do you need to repent of and turn from?

❖ How does the power of the Holy Spirit help you keep from sinning?

Write a prayer repenting of sin and thanking God for making you His child:

_____

_____

_____

*A*nd the Holy Spirit helps us in our distress. For we don't even know what we should pray for, nor how we should pray. But the Holy Spirit prays for us with groanings that cannot be expressed in words. And the Father who knows all hearts knows what the Spirit is saying, for the Spirit pleads for us believers in harmony with God's own will *(Rom. 8:26–27).*

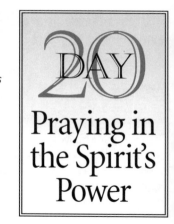

DAY 20
Praying in the Spirit's Power

In our own strength, we can only pray, "Lord be merciful to me a sinner." But in the power of the Spirit, we can ask anything in the name of Jesus (John 15:16).

When the Holy Spirit prays through us He goes way beyond our human ability to express what He desires in human words. The Holy Spirit may pray through us with tongues or groanings that go deeper than mere words. He intercedes in us for our needs, and through us for the needs of others.

When the Spirit of God uses us to pray for others (intercession), we become God's vessel for implementing His will in their lives. How? God responds to prayer because it is His ordained vehicle for implementing His will on the earth. That's why Jesus teaches us, "I also tell you this: If two of you agree down here on earth concerning anything you ask, my Father in heaven will do it for you" (Matt. 18:19).

Ephesians 6:18 gives us guidance concerning how we are to intercede for others. Read this verse now, then complete the following sentences as they relate to you after each of Paul's instructions:

Pray at all times.

Daily I pray _____.

The times I need to pray are_____.

Pray on every occasion.

What circumstances prompt you to pray immediately?_____.

In what situations do you need to be praying? _____.

Pray in the power of the Holy Spirit.

What demonstrations of the Spirit's power have you witnessed as a result of

prayer?_____.

List all the ways the Spirit prays through you:_____
_____
_____.

Be alert and persistent in your prayers.

What dangers has the Spirit alerted you to pray about? _____
_____.

What needs of others has the Spirit alerted you to pray for?_____
_____.

In what ways is the Spirit teaching you to be more patient and persistent in your praying?_____
_____.

Pray for all Christians everywhere.

What believers are you to pray for in your city, in the nation, and in the world?
_____.

How has the Spirit been leading you to pray for all Christians?_____
_____.

Ask Yourself . . .

❖ What changes in your prayer life does the Spirit desire you to make?

❖ When you pray in the power of the Spirit, what evidences of His power do you see in your life, your family, and your church?

Write a prayer of intercession the Holy Spirit desires you to pray:

_____
_____
_____
_____

*W*e have proved ourselves by our purity, our understanding, our patience, our kindness, our sincere love, and the power of the Holy Spirit [holiness of the Spirit] (2 Cor. 6:6).

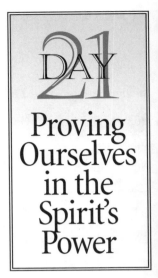

Proving Ourselves in the Spirit's Power

The integrity of any Christian ministry will be confirmed by the power of the Holy Spirit. But notice that the *power* of the Spirit is not the only confirmation. The proof of a Spirit-led ministry will first be proven by its purity (holiness), understanding (of the Word and the needs of others), kindness, and sincere (*agape*) love.

So, let's examine first things first. Before power comes purity, understanding, patience, kindness, and love. Put an *x* on the line of each of these qualities indicating where you are spiritually right now:

I am . . .

Pure and holy   Impure

Understanding the Word   Not in God's Word

Patient   Impatient

Kind   Insensitive

Loving   Hateful

The Holy Spirit works in our lives to mature God's holiness in us (2 Cor. 7:1).

> *The Spirit uses broken, pure, and holy vessels for ministry.*

The Holy Spirit may sovereignly minister through you to others, sometimes in spite of you. But to be used regularly by the Holy Spirit, you must be pure and holy and bearing the Spirit's fruit.

The Spirit manifests and proves His power through holy vessels with miraculous signs and wonders. "These signs will accompany those who believe: They will cast out demons in my name, and they will speak in new languages. They will be able to handle snakes with safety, and if they drink anything poisonous, it won't hurt them. They will be able to place their hands on the sick and heal them" (Mark 16:17–18).

Below is a list of signs and wonders taken from Mark 16 and Acts 1–4. Check any of these proofs of the Spirit's power you have witnessed in your life and church:

- ❏ The lost being saved
- ❏ Miracles
- ❏ Sick being healed
- ❏ Demons being cast out
- ❏ Speaking in tongues
- ❏ People being baptized and filled with the Holy Spirit
- ❏ Preaching the Gospel with boldness
- ❏ Other: _____

The Holy Spirit wants to give proof of His presence in your life by demonstrating His power. But we can quench and hinder Him (1 Thess. 5:19) with fear, unconfessed sin, holding onto offenses, disobedience, and unwillingness to risk.

Ask Yourself . . .

❖ Is anything in your life hindering the Spirit's power? If so, what is it? Will you confess and surrender it completely to the Holy Spirit?

❖ In what ways have you recently witnessed the Spirit's power proving His presence in your life?

Write a prayer asking for Holy Spirit's proof of holiness and powerful signs and wonders to flow in and through your life:

_____

_____

_____

_____

*H*ave you lost your senses? After starting your Christian lives in the Spirit, why are you now trying to become perfect by your own human effort? (Gal. 3:3).

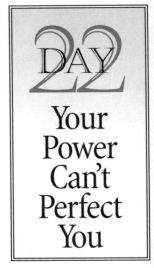

Your Power Can't Perfect You

Experiencing the power of the Spirit-led life can become intoxicating. But as we experience the Spirit's moving, the temptation always exists to believe that we can minister in signs and wonders under our own strength. Or, we may develop a spiritual arrogance that begins to inflict legalism on other Christians so they measure up to our "holier than thou" standards of piety.

The Galatians experienced the grace and power of the Holy Spirit. But they had also succumbed to the temptation of trusting in legalism instead of God's grace.They were trying to become perfect in their own efforts just as many church generations since them have done. So below is a self-test. Answer each question with a *T* for true or an *F* for false as they apply to you.

_____I take pride in my spiritual discipline.

_____I feel good when others praise me for my ministry in the gifts.

_____I look for public and highly visible opportunities to use my spiritual gifts.

_____I find myself ministering in the gifts and power of the Spirit without first seeking the leading of God's Spirit.

_____I look for gratitude from others when I minister to them.

_____I operate in the gifts whenever I choose.

If you found yourself marking any of the above statements true, you are treading upon thin ice spiritually. Because anytime we usurp the sovereignty of the Holy Spirit in our lives and ministry, we are reverting back to legalism and religious traditions that quench the Holy Spirit.

The only way to stop operating in our own efforts to begin moving again in the power of the Spirit is to repent of our sin. There must be the confession of our pride, arrogance, and legalistic attitudes, and ungodly actions. Pray the following prayer of repentance if vanity and arrogance is stifling your life.

Almighty God, I repent of trying to grow spiritually through my own efforts. I repent of the sins of spiritual arrogance and pride. And I ask for

Your forgiveness and mercy. Cleanse me with the blood of Jesus. Purge me with the fire of Your Spirit. Crucify all pride and legalism in my life. In Jesus' name, Amen.

We will always face the temptation to manipulate the Spirit instead of surrendering to His desires. Therefore, we must always be ready to receive whatever correction, teaching, and conviction the Holy Spirit has for us through His Word, prayer, prophecy, and the fellowship of the saints.

Because we never stop needing the Spirit of grace to work pride and human effort out of our lives, complete the following sentences:

The greatest spiritual temptation I face is _____

_____.

I become spiritually arrogant when _____

_____.

I need to humble myself and repent of _____

_____.

Ask Yourself . . .

❖ Is there any area of your walk in the Spirit in which you are trying to perfect yourself through your own efforts? Is so, what is it? Will you repent?

❖ How will you stay alert to avoiding the temptation to become spiritually arrogant in the future?

Write a prayer asking the Holy Spirit to convict you whenever you move from His grace to your own plans and pursuits:

_____

_____

_____

_____

_____

*B*ut when you are directed by the Holy Spirit, you are no longer subject to the law (Gal. 5:18).

DAY

Directed
by the
Spirit

The direction of by the Holy Spirit involves His convicting, teaching, and empowering of our lives in His ways. First, we need to be convicted of sin and moved to repentance. Next, we need the Holy Spirit to teach us His Word and ways. Finally, we need His power to do what He directs.

The Spirit-led life goes beyond the commandments of law. The Law can tell us what we should or shouldn't do, but without the Spirit we are powerless to obey it. The Holy Spirit does use the Law to convict us of sin and to teach us about righteousness, so the Law is good. But the Law can't save us.

Read Romans 7:14–25 then answer the following questions:

1. What is the purpose of the Law?_____
_____.

2. What does obedience to the Law accomplish?_____
_____.

3. What happens when we try to do what is right? _____
_____.

4. How is our slavery to sin overcome? _____
_____.

> *The Holy Spirit directs our lives through Scripture, prayer, prophecy, and the fellowship of the saints.*

All the Holy Spirit teaches and speaks to us must conform to the Word of God. Any thought or word that contradicts God's Word is not from the Holy Spirit (1 John 4:1–6).

Describe a time in your life when the Holy Spirit directed your life in a direction that seemed foolish or impossible at the time but later proved to be the perfect will of God for you:

_____

_____

_____

The Holy Spirit empowers you to do the right thing, at the right time, for the right reason, with the right words and actions. Is there a situation you are facing right now that needs the guidance and direction of the Holy Spirit? If so, begin praying for His direction. Ask the Holy Spirit to reveal to you through His Word, prayer, prophecy, and the fellowship of the saints these answers. As you receive from Him, write down the Spirit's directions:

Holy Spirit, concerning _____**reveal to me:**

1. What is the right thing to do?

2. When shall I do it?

3. How should I feel and what motive should I have?

4. What words and actions do You desire me to take?

Never get ahead of the direction of the Spirit. You can do the right thing at the wrong time and grieve Him (Eph. 4:20). So seek His Word, His Way, His power, and His timing, to do what is right for His glory.

Ask Yourself . . .

❖ Where do you need the direction of His Spirit right now?

❖ Are you staying in His Word, Way, timing, and power for His glory?

Write a prayer asking Jesus to direct you at all times through the power of the Holy Spirit:

_____

_____

_____

_____

_____

*T*hose who live only to satisfy their own sinful desires will harvest the consequences of decay and death. But those who live to please the Spirit will harvest everlasting life from the Spirit (Gal. 6:8).

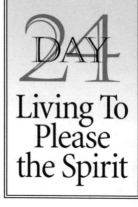

DAY 24
Living To Please the Spirit

If we sow according to the Spirit, we will reap life. But, if we sow sin, we will reap destruction and death. The law of sowing and reaping is one of the simplest truths in Scripture. We will reap what we sow.

If we are to live a life pleasing to the Spirit, we need to know what pleases God. So read the following verses then jot down what they reveal about pleasing the Lord:

Leviticus 8:28 _____

Deuteronomy 12:28, 13:18 _____

Psalm 19:13–14; 69:30–31 _____

Micah 6:7–8 _____

Romans 14:8–10, 17–18 _____

2 Corinthians 5:1–15 _____

Philippians 2:13 _____

Colossians 3:20 _____

1 Timothy 2:1–3; 5:4 _____

Hebrews 11:5–6 _____

Galatians 6:7 warns us *not to be deceived* about sowing and reaping. Deceived about what? Time. Why time? Because the results or consequences of sin are not always immediate. In fact, sin may bring temporary pleasure in the natural. But the seeds of sin's sowing will bring an eventual harvest of pain and destruction. The difficulty of sowing to the Spirit is that the short-term consequences may be difficult and painful. But the Spirit's reward is long-term . . . eternal.

Below is a list of actions that sow to either sin, or to the Spirit. Write down the short-term and long-term consequences of their harvest.

Action	Short-term Harvest	Long-term Harvest
Abstinence	_____	_____
Fornication	_____	_____

Abortion _____ _____

Lying _____ _____

Honesty · _____ _____

Stealing _____ _____

Obeying _____ _____

Giving _____ _____

Now think of ways you can sow to the Spirit. List three ways below and their long-term harvest:

Sowing to the Spirit	Harvest
1._____	_____
2._____	_____
3._____	_____

> *When we live to please the Spirit, we discover the lasting rewards of life filled with His joy and peace.*

Even if there is temporary suffering, trials, or persecution, the eternal rewards of obedience far surpass any good gift we could think of or imagine (Eph. 3:14–19).

Ask Yourself . . .

❖ What are you sowing to now that won't bring an eternal harvest? Is it worth doing? When will you stop?

❖ What will you sow today into the Spirit for an eternal harvest?

Write a prayer asking God's Spirit for wisdom in sowing and reaping:

_____

_____

_____

_____

I *have never stopped thanking God for you. I pray for you constantly, asking God, the glorious Father of our Lord Jesus Christ, to give you spiritual wisdom and understanding, so that you might grow in your knowledge of God (Eph. 1:16–17).*

DAY 25

The Spirit's Wisdom

Living the Spirit-led life requires godly wisdom. So Paul is literally praying in this passage for the Ephesians to receive the Spirit of wisdom. Jesus is the wisdom of God (1 Cor. 1) and He gives us His Spirit. All we have to do is ask: "If you need wisdom—if you want to know what God wants you to do—ask him, and he will gladly tell you. He will not resent your asking" (James 1:5).

> *Wisdom is seeing all of life from God's perspective, not ours.*

Wisdom is knowing, understanding, and doing what God wants.

Take some time to read Proverbs chapters 8 and 9. As you do, write in the left column all the qualities of wisdom, and in the right column the benefits that come from being wise in God's Spirit:

Wisdom is . . .

The blessings of wisdom are . . .

_____   _____

_____   _____

_____   _____

_____   _____

_____   _____

_____   _____

The Spirit of wisdom invites us to grow in our knowledge of God, enabling an intimate, personal relationship with Him. So the Holy Spirit empowers us to draw closer to God— which gives us the Father's perspective and view of life. When we're close to His mind and heart, we think and feel as He does. We walk in His wisdom.

Paul writes in 1 Corinthians 1:18–19 that the wisdom of God appears as foolishness to unredeemed, fallen humanity. Below is a list of things from that chapter that Paul says the world sees as foolish. Jot down next to them why they are truly wisdom from the Spirit's perspective:

The cross seems foolish but shows God's wisdom: _____

_____

Preaching seems foolish but is used in God's wisdom: _____

_____

The Resurrection seems foolish but is wisdom because: _____

_____

God chose things despised by the world to show that: _____

_____

God's plan, which seemed foolish, was wise because: _____

_____

Ask Yourself . . .

❖ What are you seeing from a human perspective that you need to see through the wisdom of God's Spirit?

❖ How has the Spirit of wisdom changed your view of yourself? Your family? Your church? The lost?

Write a prayer asking God for the Spirit of wisdom to anoint you with His knowledge and understanding:

_____

_____

_____

_____

_____

I pray that from his glorious, unlimited resources he will give you mighty inner strength through his Holy Spirit (Eph. 3:16).

DAY 26

Mighty Inner Strength Through the Spirit

Two sets of words don't belong together in any Christian's vocabulary when God's will is to be done. They are: *I can't,* and, *It's impossible.* The truth is that God never requires us to do anything that we can't do through the power of His Spirit. "It is not by force nor by strength, but by my Spirit, says the LORD Almighty" (Zech. 4:6).

Take some time to discover the promises of strength and miracle-working power that come through the Holy Spirit. Below is a set of barbells. Write over them all the ways God strengthens us: (Zech. 4:6; Phil. 4:13; 2 Cor. 12:8–10; Matt. 19:26; Mark 9:23, 20:27; Luke 1:37, 18:27; Ps. 23:3, 118:14, 138:3; Isa. 40:29–31)

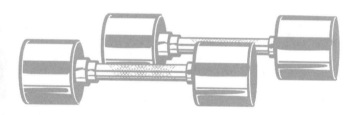

Spiritual strength is built when we exercise our faith. The Holy Spirit inspires faith in us as we exercise our faithfulness to Christ. But how does He do that?

The Holy Spirit uses trials and tests to strengthen our faith. Read 1 Peter 1:1–7 then write a sentence describing how God's Spirit will use trials to strengthen you:

_____

_____

> *When we stop trying and start trusting Him,*
> *the Holy Spirit empowers us to live for Christ.*

But when we try to make things happen spiritually, we suffer disappointing results and tragic failure.

Consider the example of Samson. Read how the Holy Spirit strengthened him in the following scriptures, then jot down what the Spirit did through Samson's strength:

Judges 14:6 _____

Judges 14:19 _____

Judges 15:14 _____

When Samson tried to do things his way and in his own strength, he was defeated and enslaved by the enemy.

So the message of Samson is this: Rely on your own strength and the enemy can gain a foothold to harass and oppress you. But when you seek the Spirit's power, your walk will be empowered to cruise right over the enemy's head. Because: "The God of peace will soon crush Satan under your feet. May the grace of our Lord Jesus Christ be with you" (Rom. 16:20).

Ask Yourself . . .

❖ Within yourself, where do you still rely on your own strength instead of the inner strength of His Spirit?

❖ What victory are you giving God praise for today in your life?

Write a prayer thanking God for the inner strength He gives you by the power of His Spirit:

_____

_____

_____

_____

_____

P *ut on salvation as your helmet, and take the sword of the Spirit, which is the Word of God (Eph. 6:17).*

At times in the Spirit-led life, you will find yourself in the midst of spiritual warfare. Evil rulers and authorities in the unseen world will attack you. Satan will muster mighty powers of darkness against you. But you don't stand alone! You have mighty weapons: "We use God's mighty weapons, not mere worldly weapons, to knock down the Devil's strongholds" (2 Cor. 10:4).

Protecting your life is the armor of God, and each part represents a different aspect of Jesus Himself. In fact, when you put on God's armor, you put on Christ (Rom. 13:14). When you put on the armor of God (Eph. 6:10–19), you clothe yourself with the following parts: (Look up each passage and write down each aspect of Christ you are wearing in Him [Eph. 1:13]).

Belt of truth (John 14:6) _____

Breastplate or body armor of righteousness (1 Cor. 1:30) _____

Shoes of the Gospel of peace (Eph. 2:14; Isa. 9:6) _____

Shield of faith (Rom. 5:1) _____

Helmet of salvation (1 Cor. 2:16; Rom. 10:9–13)_____

Sword of the Spirit (Heb. 4:12; Rev. 1:16, 19:15, 21) _____

The Holy Spirit uses the sword of God's Word in our lives to defeat the enemy. Read Matthew 4, then write down how Jesus defeated the devil:

Jesus defeated the devil's temptation to turn stones into bread by:_____

_____

Jesus defeated the devil's temptation to jump from the temple by: _____

_____

Jesus defeated the devil's temptation to worship him by: _____

_____

Not only is the sword of the Spirit a devastating weapon against the enemy, the Holy Spirit uses His sword as a spiritual scalpel to do deep surgery in our lives. Read Hebrews 4:12–13, then describe the surgery God's Spirit is doing in your life with His scalpel of truth right now. Check all that apply:

❑ Exposing sin

❑ Correcting wrong doctrine or beliefs

❑ Building faith

❑ Revealing the nature of the triune God

❑ Encouraging you to minister to other

❑ Building boldness to witness

❑ Laying a foundation for praying the Word

❑ Apply the Word's truths to decisions

❑ Strengthening your walk in the Spirit

Ask Yourself . . .

❖ How does the Spirit desire to use His sword in and through you?

❖ Where do you need to use the sword of the Spirit to defeat the enemy?

Write a prayer asking God to show you the power of His sword of the Spirit to remove strongholds in your life:

_____

_____

_____

_____

_____

M ay the grace of our Lord Jesus Christ, the love of God, and the fellowship of the Holy Spirit be with you all (2 Cor. 13:13).

The fellowship (*koinonia*) of the Holy Spirit is a close abiding relationship with Him and with those who are knit together in His love (Col. 2:1–3; 1 John 1).

> *Fellowshiping in the Spirit involves drawing close to God's Spirit through His Word, prayer, ministry, and fellowshiping with other believers.*

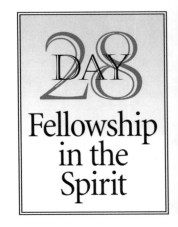

Day 28
Fellowship in the Spirit

We need one another as members of Christ's body to remain steadfast in the Spirit-led life (1 Cor. 12). Consider for a moment God's armor that we explored yesterday (Eph. 6:10–19). The word "you" and "our" appear in Ephesians 6:10–11 because we are in this fight together. In medieval times, it took other people to help a knight put on his armor. It was much too heavy and difficult to put on by one's self. Likewise, we need one another in the body of Christ to help one another in our spiritual walks.

Below are some passages that talk about what happens when Christians fellowship together in the Spirit. Read each passage, then jot down what gathering together in Jesus' name (Christian fellowship) involves:

Acts 2:1–6 _____

Acts 2:43–47 _____

Acts 4:23–31 _____

Acts 4:32–37 _____

Acts 6:1–7 _____

1 Corinthians 14:26–28 _____

Ephesians 5:15–20 _____

Colossians 3:16–17 _____

Hebrews 10:25 _____

James 5:14–20 _____

Matthew 18:15–20 _____

You may be familiar with the great sequoia trees in California. These massive trees grow to be the largest trees on earth, yet they have a very shallow root system. How is it that these mammoths can stand so strong in the winds and storms that pummel them with such shallow roots? The answer is simple. The roots of the sequoia interlock with one another so every individual tree is holding the others up. The same is true of believers who fellowship in the Holy Spirit. Each one of us holds one another up in our trials and in our joy (1 Cor. 12:26).

On the lines below, write the names of people with whom you fellowship in the Holy Spirit. Then praise God for these wonderful Christians who are there to strengthen you in every circumstance.

_____

_____

_____

_____

If you don't have loving fellowship in the Spirit with other believers, ask the Holy Spirit to guide you to the ones with whom He desires you to be.

Ask Yourself . . .

❖ How can you grow more intimate in your fellowship with the Holy Spirit?

❖ What can you do to enlarge your circle of love in the Spirit with other Christians?

Write a prayer thanking the Lord for all the opportunities you have with other Christians to fellowship in the Spirit:

_____

_____

_____

_____

_____

F *or we who worship God in the Spirit are the only ones who are truly circumcised. We put no confidence in human effort. Instead, we boast about what Jesus Christ has done for us. (Phil. 3:3) . . . For God is a Spirit, so those who worship him must worship in spirit and in truth (John 4:24).*

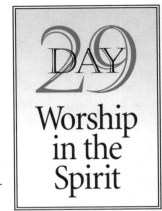

Worship in the Spirit

The Jews believed they were the only ones who could properly worship God because they were circumcised as the people of God. But the author of Hebrews rebuked such thinking, just as Jesus did, because true worship is not a matter of physical birth or effort (Jer. 4:4; Rom. 2:28–29). True worship is about the heart.

Like the Samaritans back then, humans still tend to focus on the style rather than the substance of worship. Style has to do with superficial things in worship, while substance pertains to the indwelling Spirit in our lives. Below is a list of various style and substance issues that pertain to worship. Read Psalm 149:1–3, 150; 1 Samuel 16:7; Ephesians 5:18–20; 1 Timothy 2:8; Hebrews 13:15, then put an *x* on each line defining whether that issue is one of mere human style, or of true spiritual substance.

In worship, the way . . .

One is dressed

_____
Style   Substance

One sings

_____
Style   Substance

One thinks in their heart

_____
Style   Substance

One claps or raises hands

_____
Style   Substance

One fears God

_____
Style   Substance

One responds verbally

_____
Style   Substance

One prays

_____
Style   Substance

One loves God

_____
Style   Substance

One respects leadership,
dignity, and order in worship _____

Style   Substance

When our heart is tender toward and filled with the Holy Spirit, our worship of God is true and Spirit-led. But when people are more concerned about what other people are doing, saying, and wearing, worship becomes a religious service focused on a form, not on God.

Complete the following sentences about yourself:

When I worship, I _____

_____.

What distracts me in worship is _____

_____.

I prepare for true worship by _____

_____.

In worship, I need the Holy Spirit within me to _____

_____.

Examine yourself. Be certain before you worship that you have allowed the Holy Spirit to prepare your mind and heart to enter into the presence of God. Also be careful to guard what you see and hear before worship. If you have a family, come to worship with them in love, peace, and harmony, not fighting or arguing with one another.

Ask Yourself . . .

❖ How does the Holy Spirit prepare you to worship in Spirit and truth?

❖ What distracts you from worshiping in the Spirit?

Write a prayer asking the Holy Spirit to prepare you daily for worship in Spirit and truth:

_____

_____

_____

*F*or when we brought you the Good News, it was not only with words but also with power, for the Holy Spirit gave you full assurance that what we said was true (1 Thess. 1:5).

DAY 30
Full Assurance

The good news of the Spirit-led life is that the Holy Spirit will enable you to live with power and holiness. You can be assured that He is working in you to complete His plan for your life so you can walk forward with the Holy Spirit in boldness and confidence (Phil. 1:6).

At times, you won't fully understand why the Spirit is directing you in a certain way. But you can rest knowing that His plan for your life is for your very best (Jer. 29:11–12).

Complete these sentences:

In the Spirit, I am most confident of _____

_____.

Where I lack confidence in the Holy Spirit is _____

_____.

My prayer for confidence is _____

_____.

Take some time now to reflect back over what you have learned in this study. Remember all the different ways you have encountered the Holy Spirit in your study, Bible reading, and prayers. Then complete the following:

1. For me, being led by the Spirit means _____

_____.

2. One area of my life that has grown in spiritual maturity during this devotional study is _____.

_____.

3. When I am intimate with the Spirit, I _____

_____.

4. The Holy Spirit is directing me to _____

_____.

5. The Holy Spirit is empowering me to _____

_____.

6. The Holy Spirit is teaching me _____

_____.

7. The Holy Spirit is convicting me of _____

_____.

8. The Holy Spirit is counseling me to _____

_____.

9. The Holy Spirit is comforting me in _____

_____.

10. The Holy Spirit is leading me to _____

_____.

Ask Yourself . . .

❖ Are you willing to surrender everything in your life to the control and leading of the Holy Spirit?

❖ With whom will you share the joys of the Spirit-led life?

Write a prayer asking the Holy Spirit to lead you every moment of your life:

_____

_____

_____

_____

_____

You can continue your encounters with the Holy Spirit by using the other devotional study guides listed at the end of this booklet, and by using the companion *Holy Spirit Encounter Bible.*

Leader's Guide

For Group Sessions

This devotional study is an excellent resource for group study including such settings as:

- ❖ Sunday school classes and other church classes.
- ❖ Prayer groups.
- ❖ Bible study groups.
- ❖ Ministries involving small groups, home groups, and accountability groups.
- ❖ Study groups for youth and adults.

Before the first session

- ❖ Contact everyone interested or already participating in the group about the meeting time, date, and place.
- ❖ Make certain that everyone has a copy of *Living the Spirit-led Life.*
- ❖ Ask group members to begin their daily encounters in this guide. While each session will not strictly adhere to a seven-day schedule, group members who faithfully do a devotional each day will be prepared to share in the group sessions. Plan out all your sessions before starting the first session.
- ❖ Pray for the Holy Spirit to guide, teach, and help each participant.
- ❖ Be certain that the place where you will meet has a chalkboard, white board, or flipchart with appropriate writing materials. It is also best to be in a setting with movable seating.

Planning the Group Sessions

1. You will have four sessions together as a group. So plan to cover at least seven days in each session. If your sessions are weekly, then have your group members complete the final two days prior to your last session.

2. In your first session, have group members find a partner to be the person with whom they share and pray during each session. Keep the same pairs throughout the group sessions. You can randomly put pairs together—men with men and women with women.

3. Begin each session with prayer.

4. Read or ask group members to read the key Scriptures at the start of each daily devotional for the seven days prior to that session.

5. As the leader, decide which exercises and questions you would like to cover from the seven daily devotional studies prior to the group session.

6. Decide which exercises and sessions will be most appropriate for your group to share as a whole and which would be more comfortable for group members to share in pairs.

7. From the seven previous days, decide which prayer(s) you wish the pairs to pray with one another.

8. Close each session with each group member sharing with the total group how he or she encountered the Holy Spirit during the previous week, then lead the group in prayer or have group members pray aloud in a circle of prayer before you close the session.

9. In the last session, you will have nine previous days to share. Use the last day as an in-depth sharing time in pairs. Invite all the group members to share the most important thing they learned about the Holy Spirit during the study, and how their relationship with the Spirit was deepened because of it. Close with prayers of praise and thanksgiving.

10. Remember that in sharing either in pairs or the total group to allow each person the freedom not to share if they aren't comfortable.

11. Always start and end the group session on time and seek to keep the session to no longer than ninety minutes. And finally, be careful. This is not a therapy group. Group members who seek to dominate group discussions with their own problems or questions should be ministered to by the group leader or pastor one on one outside of the group session.

Titles in the Holy Spirit
Encounter Guide Series

Additional Notes

Additional Notes

Additional Notes

Additional Notes

Additional Notes

Additional Notes